Letter to My Husband

Letter to My Husband

NOTES ABOUT MOURNING AND RECOVERY

Jill Truman

VIKING

VIKING
Viking Penguin Inc., 40 West 23rd Street,
New York, New York 10010, U.S.A.
Penguin Books Ltd, Harmondsworth,
Middlesex, England
Penguin Books Australia Ltd, Ringwood,
Victoria, Australia
Penguin Books Canada Limited, 2801 John Street,
Markham, Ontario, Canada L3R 1B4
Penguin Books (N.Z.) Ltd, 182–190 Wairau Road,
Auckland 10, New Zealand

First published in 1987 by Viking Penguin Inc.
Published simultaneously in Canada

LIBRARY OF CONGRESS CATALOGING IN PUBLICATION DATA
Truman, Jill.
Letter to my husband.
1. Bereavement—Psychological aspects. 2. Grief.
3. Truman, Jill—Diaries. 4. Widows—United States—
Diaries. I. Title.
BF575.G7T78   1987   155.9'37   86-40497
ISBN 0-670-81760-0

Printed in the United States of America by
Murray Printing Company, Westford, Massachusetts
Set in Weiss and Caslon 471
Designed by Anne Winslow

For Annaliese, Crispin,
Nadya, and Rebecca

I will keep faith with death in my heart. . . .
for the sake of goodness, for the sake of love,
let no man's heart be ruled by death.
—Thomas Mann

Letter to My Husband

My dear love, tomorrow it will be exactly four months since you died. It seems like forty years that I have been battling on alone, and yet your presence is so vivid that I expect at any moment to hear your key turn in the lock and your loud familiar voice calling "hello," as you stride along the hallway. With what joy would we all rush to greet you, because no man was ever more loved than you, you old bastard. The children would wake up and come tumbling down the stairs—yes, even Annaliese who learnt to climb up the stairs and then to slither rapidly down backwards, just a few days after you died. How clever for ten months. How I wanted you to see her.

She was ten months old on the day you died and such a baby—you wouldn't recognise the confident little girl who scuttles round on hands and feet, bottom in the air. And, heartbreak, she has forgotten you. Someone gave her a baby-walker truck the other day, and just this evening she discovered the joy of walking around pushing it. Then she messed her pants and had to be changed. She's not all sweetness and light.

Can you see any of this, I wonder? What does it mean to be dead? I cannot accept that you are totally annihilated. All that passion, all that restless striving and enthusiasm—gone? Nothing left but a little box of ashes? No. No. No, my dearest love. I often feel your presence so powerfully. The only moments of happiness I have experienced in the past few months have been those when I felt that you were near. Am I deluding myself? Is it a defence mechanism, can I not accept the reality? Or are you really somewhere and trying to bring me a little peace of mind? I worry about your well-being. Are you happy? Do you still suffer from angst? Can you see us all and do you think I am doing the right things? If only I knew. Not that a disembodied spirit is much help to someone who is longing for your physical warmth and touch and smell. But if you are a happy disembodied spirit, my very physical sweetheart, then I would be content for you and bear it as well as I can.

I spend a lot of time thinking about all this, and trying to formulate some new philosophy of life. But I don't come up with any answers. None of the religions seem to be of any help—unless I could take a leap across the chasm of blind faith to the far side where all certainties are clearly mapped out. I have read three books about spiritualism, but the writers could be as deluded as the religious ones. All I really want to know is whether you are "all right."

Because, my darling, I love you as much now as I ever did. Ridiculous to be so romantic after all those years of marriage. And we had so much more in front of us, so much uncompleted. So many things to discuss and work through in our relationship. And four beautiful children.

* * *

Tonight I am exhausted—physically, mentally, emotionally. I long all day for these few moments when I can write to you before I go to sleep. But I have to work so very hard just to keep us going that I am too tired to write down even a small part of that complex of feelings and incidents that I want you to know about. That is what I have done since you died, mostly: hard physical labour. Most of it is necessary, but some of it is compulsive—a way of fighting, or perhaps avoiding, grief and despair.

Loneliness is what most bereaved people complain of, but I can't say that I have ever felt lonely. In fact, I often long for just a few hours to be alone with my grief, indulge it almost. Friends from far and near have called in. The comfort of knowing that people care is very great. I was delighted to see each dear person who made the effort—fancy, they really cared about what had happened to us! But how much I wanted them all to go away. How many of them realised, I wonder, that most of the time they were talking to a mask? A very careful mock-up of what used to be my personality. While the real me, the new me, waited, tense and only just in control, in the wings, ready to rush to the centre of the stage the minute they were gone.

Why this schizophrenia? I don't suppose anyone would have minded if I had shrieked and yelled and groaned. It was just that I could not.

So everyone thinks that I'm calm and strong and competent, when in fact I'm just a battered, tattered muddle. So what? What matters is you. I must know what has happened to you. That hideous thing that lay dying was not the last of my strong and arrogant, my handsome husband. My soul revolts at the thought. And what was it that you indicated so often in the middle distance beyond your hospital bed? If only we could have communicated. Knowing that you were dying, I thought it was perhaps some vision of "death."

I can read now. For about three months, reading was a near-impossibility. But now that I can, I must try to read some philosophy, try to understand what it has all been about, and whether it means anything and leads anywhere.

I originally thought of writing to you when you had been dead for only a week or two. I remember the moment. You know how we almost always had Sunday morning tea, all six of us, in our bed? The patchwork quilt, finished after so many years, is now *in situ*. I finished the last few patches with a heavy heart, knowing that you would never sleep under it. Anyway, to the point: One Sunday, there sat Nadya, amid the chaos of bed and bodies, not quite seven years old, in her blue kaftan, concentrating so hard on trying to read the Sunday paper. She was so

6

much her little serious self. Just a few short weeks before, you and I would have exchanged a smiling glance of love over her head. I thought: I must tell him about it, I must write it down.

C.S. Lewis did a similar thing on the death of his wife. Recently, I read the resulting book hungrily, hoping for some prop or guide. But, apart from a small wavering, he believes that God exists and Christianity is the true faith, and that his wife is therefore okay. I can fathom no reason, except perhaps the cultural and historical, for accepting this premise. He says also that grief is like fear. It is not. Grief is a physical pain. In the breast. I didn't know that before. He writes, too, that he could not speak about his wife to his children, because of the embarrassment they felt. Embarrassment! Never fear, my love, we talk about you all the time, have wept together for you and laughed about you. And we will tell Annaliese all about you when she is big enough to understand.

Rebecca was distraught at first. I thought that

she would never be able to control herself. She loves you so strongly and with an uncomplicated, child's love. Crispin was very quiet and introverted for a while, and I don't really know what he was feeling. He takes his responsibilities as the eldest very seriously. Nadya, your little treasure, seemed unaffected for some weeks— hard-hearted little bitch, I thought. But she was too young for ordinary grief, and has recently posed me a lot of psychological problems.

They have all rallied round me, and give me support that, if I were an outsider, I would say was a tribute to their upbringing so far. But, as I am an insider and know that we brought them up ordinarily and sometimes badly, I can only accept gratefully and with some surprise.

I cleared part of the garage today. I have to dispose of so many of your treasured bits and pieces, kept for years in case they should come in useful. Forgive me, darling. I have to work so hard already just to keep going, I can't ever become a handyman on your scale as well. I have mastered a bit of necessary carpentry and electrical maintenance. I hate doing it. Like throwing away your toothbrush and packing up your clothes, I feel as though I am kicking you out. There are many things I can't part with. But what are things? They don't bring you back and I must simplify my life so that I don't have to work flat out for ever. Even now, I know that I must start a new life some day and that there must be time for pleasure in it.

But you are so much part of me. Which of my attitudes and thought processes can be considered wholly mine after so long an association with yours? Our life together has been a turmoil. But I'm glad that we did so much, together. How much of it would I have done alone? Less? More? God knows when I shall have the spirit for expeditions, adventures, rows even, again.

I'm exhausted again tonight, but still I scribble on instead of sleeping. It's worst of all when I'm menstruating, the grief and the weariness. I hardly bleed at all—a few drops each month. Doctor says it's normal in the circumstances. But I feel just as bad—no, much worse—than when I'm having a normal period.

It's funny writing about periods to someone who isn't even breathing or eating. Can disembodied spirits understand these very physical problems?

There are some nights when I can't write. Nothing is possible but grief.

The sun shone today and it has been warm and springlike after a period of real cold and wet. Impossible not to feel a lightening of the heart. A beautiful clear starry night when I went for my usual nighttime stroll in the garden. That is when I say good night to you. Are you really there in the garden at nighttime? And in the early morning? I always find myself foolishly smiling when I feel that you are around. Am I madder or more sane than our many friends who would laugh to read this?

Certainly I am more poignantly aware of the beauties of nature. I cry out for you to see them with me. Particularly the sky. One reason for not going back to Manchester. I feel a need for beauty on the doorstep, not a rare and fraught car ride away. Yet when you were alive I longed to return to our Manchester life. What do I want for what remains of our family? What would you want? I shall have to leave here. It tears at my heart to say so. All our plans for this place must be abandoned, although in deciding that, I feel that I am abandoning you. But, if I did complete them, supposing I had the will, energy, time, money—what then? The home of our dreams without you? But I don't want to leave here because you are everywhere in this house. And I love you.

Annaliese caught her tiny fingers in the front door today. At first I thought they were crushed, but they were only badly cut. How she screamed! Her first experience of real pain. If you could see her, how she has grown and developed.

Crispin has been off school with what seems to be more bronchitis than asthma. He bears it very patiently.

I must go to sleep now. I looked in the mirror today and saw a tired old hag. So what? That's what I am.

Just been tarting up the old hag. Funny how vanity begins to reassert itself. I don't like to admit that my looks are fading and I have to be in a very bad way to neglect my appearance for more than a day or two.

Rebecca left Joseph in his outside pen last night. Today he had vanished. I suppose a cat or a dog got him. Becca wept quite a lot, but nothing like she wept at the death of her first guinea pig, or even when the first goldfish died, five years ago. She has known real tragedy since then.

We played the new record player (wired up and carpentered into the bookcase by clever me—*and* I put the new parts on the carpet sweeper) last Saturday. Nadya refused to listen. She begged me, tearfully, to stay in the kitchen with her until the records were over. She couldn't bear the music without you. It's so dull here now. I wonder if I'll ever feel that zest for life and movement again. I just feel tired all the time.

It's a funny thing, grief. I haven't felt it at all today. Just tired.

We all went to the library today. As I drove out of the car park, I saw this man who resembled you. I just stopped and watched him approach. Just looked and looked, possessed by the stupid hope that I could somehow turn him into you by an effort of will. The closer he approached, the less he resembled you. He must have thought I was behaving strangely. There are not many men as tall and handsome as you, my love. I didn't appreciate you properly.

Maude was here tonight. Your death was a real blow to her. You had far more friends among women than among men—I mean real friends. She thinks that people's personalities continue to exist as long as they are remembered. If she is right, this puts a terrible responsibility on me, because I am the only person who can approach the knowledge of your entire personality. But even I only understood you partially. And in memory your existence is even less perfect. Am I remembering you as better or worse than the reality? I try not to be selective in my recollections, but how can I be otherwise? Whether I am remembering your kindnesses or your cruelties, the knife wound is the same. A lot of the time I just ache, ache, ache for you, without recalling any particular mood or characteristic. Perhaps, after all, that is what counts—the warmth and comfort of your presence, the essential you which was always there to love, to shout at, to help, to call upon in time of need. Now quite gone.

Every night, these lovely clear nights, the moon is a little larger and my life with you just a little bit farther away. Little by little you are slipping away from me, and all the love in my heart cannot hold you.

If, if you are "all right," won't you let me know, my darling? I believe I could build a new life for us all if I felt at peace about your well-being. Often I am crawling about in this pit of misery, but I haul myself out again. Unless there are further disasters, we'll manage. We'll long for you, but we'll manage. But how about you? Are you happy, you restless, angst-ridden creature? I WANT TO KNOW. I want to help you.

~~~~~~~

This is very irregular! It is halfway through the afternoon, and I only allow myself to write to you at night. But I suppose it is better than retreating to the whisky bottle. I have been packing up for a holiday. We have been lent a cottage in Snowdonia. It will be lovely and I don't suppose we would have gone if you had been here. Holidays, holidays, holidays, before the children were born and since, all parts of the world, with or without a tent. The excitements, panics, rows. I suppose that I thought it would go on for ever. Last year we took our lovely new tiny baby and camped in rainy Normandy. If we had known it would be our last holiday, where would we have gone? Remember Annaliese lying on her tummy in the carrycot in the tent, beaming happily up at us all? Me breastfeeding her while the rains sluiced down and dripped through the holes? You said she was the only one of us who didn't run off and leave you. . . .

What a silly bitch I am, sitting here crying instead of being grateful that we are having a holiday. I have been remembering those last few hours at the hospital, as you lay unconscious, hideous, dying. They said you wouldn't have been the same man if you had lived, and my reason tells me that death was better than that and it would have been terrible for all of us. But my heart wants you, in any form, just you, unique you.

Full moon tonight, my love. Tomorrow it will begin to wane and it will be full again and again and again and every time you will be further away from me. I panic sometimes in case I forget how you looked, moved, spoke. I must remember every detail. But I can't just remember you as you were five months ago. You developed into that person from the skinny student I first knew and loved. Always the same and always changing. I too, I suppose. As time progressed, we would have gone on changing together. But now I shall sink into middle and old age alone, while you, suddenly cut off with so much before you, will remain always young. I am glad that I shall not see you old, Love. And you won't see me old and ugly, will you? Good. How would you have been two years, five years, twenty years hence? How would I have been if you had not died? Already I have started to become different. I am thinner, forced to be more practical, to understand everything, to be in charge all the time, day and night, to comfort the grieving children, to be competent outside, and a bleeding, screaming mess inside.

The journey tomorrow frightens me. I am terrified of dying for one reason only—the children. Otherwise, I would be so glad to die.

A week since I wrote anything. Managed the journey to North Wales and back. I must try to remain alive until Crispin is, say, about twenty. They are able children and would, I think, manage with advice and assistance from the Blacks. They would stick together. Ideally, I ought to survive until Annaliese is about twenty—nineteen years more. After that, they won't need me.

The holiday was a great success for all of us. The children are all better in health and spirits, even Nadya (who is still unwell in both, however). Our little scrap discovered her legs and insisted on walking at her tediously slow pace whenever possible. She is an extremely "good" child, fits in with whatever we want to do quite happily, but just occasionally asserts her will with great firmness in a way which reminds me so vividly of you. I still worry about all your problems. All my questions remain unanswered.

All week, while on holiday, I've stopped wondering. And only once was I seized by uncontrollable grief: suddenly and quite unreasonably I felt that I was responsible for your death, and began to sob and cried out aloud. A madness which passed quite quickly. What causes it? Perhaps because sometimes when you were driving me mad, I wished you would just drop dead?

Why is it that everything they all say, all the people I meet, unless it is about you or on the subject of death, is so uninteresting? I read a little now, but hardly ever watch TV or play a record. Apart from lack of interest, I'm so very busy. But at least people have stopped constantly coming to see if I'm all right. I was always touched, but it was a terrible strain.

In a way, I'm glad to be home again. I feel almost lighthearted: You aren't dead, I'm just writing to you abroad somewhere, and in a few nights' time I'll be sleeping in your arms.

I had such a lovely dream last night, so vivid that I have been recalling it with pleasure all day.

How beautifully I used to sleep in your arms. The most truly happy moments of marriage, perhaps of life, were those last few moments before falling asleep. Never again. It's hard to bear. Is it harder for me, who has to carry on, or for you, who are dead?

The dream took place in Beaumaris Castle. You were suddenly there beside me and I held one of your beautiful hands in both of mine. I shouted out with joy that I could feel it, really feel your lovely warm hand. Then you went off, slowly, up one of the stone stairways, cheerfully. And I knew that you were truly dead and that I would never see you again.

I have been much better since the holiday. The face in the mirror is not so tired and drawn and I feel that I am coping better. I was at a very low point before we went away; the burden of grieving was almost too much. It was a good holiday—better because of the physical hardships, perhaps. And I did not miss you all the time, having the honesty to admit to myself that it would not have gone so smoothly with my restless, willful, discontented spouse around.

The children often discuss my imminent birthday, and what they are going to buy me. Rebecca said this morning that she often daydreams that she asks me what I want, and I say "Daddy," and she gives him to me. I asked, "Where do you get him from?" She replied, "He comes floating down through the ceiling." Hard to imagine my very solid lover floating ethereally.

⁓

Coldest June day since records began. The weather is in mourning for you, my love. We could all do with some sunshine. In the evenings I become quite stiff with cold. Central heating bills are a worry, so I don't turn it on. Cold and clear and starry outside, so I hurried in. Am I beginning to forget? Grow scar tissue? Certainly, in the mountain air last week, life seemed worth living again, and I forgot to grieve for longish periods. But I am no nearer to formulating any philosophy of life or death.

——

If the children are your only form of immortality, I have a terrific responsibility to bring them up, not only to be splendid and happy people, but also to remember you clearly. Some things would already please you: the way they have rallied round in these past months. Annaliese enjoys music, beams with delight when one of them plays the piano. Crispin handles the motor-mower more competently than I do. Rebecca is growing quite beautiful, confident, and charming and shows signs of being a goodish flautist. Crispin passed the eleven-plus (my first thought was that you would have been pleased). Nadya is a little enigma. Her personality has changed completely since you died. It worries me that I don't understand her.

I noticed today that the calendar in the music room is still on April. You would not have allowed that to happen! Many things have changed: culinary standards have plummeted, we have fewer rows and less merriment. Life is duller.

Whatever form of immortality you may or may not have attained, I have to accept that your dear body has gone forever. That's hard to bear: not only the warmth and comfort and passion it afforded me, but also its actual existence. I often recall it. I dwell on the way you walked, gestured, frowned, smiled. I can see the sheen on your forehead, the cut on your left wrist, the funny nail on the fourth finger of your right hand. Your long, lovely hands, your knees, the curve of your tummy, the hairs on your bottom. I hope that you will always remain so physically vivid. Don't go away, my love.

It can't all have been for nothing, that unique body, soul, mind. I have lived for you. I don't want to live without you. I can't.

One wonderful bonus. The last articulate thing you said to me: "I love you very much." Whatever made you take my hand and say that, in pain as you were, on that first night at the hospital? Little did either of us realise that you would never be able to speak properly again. How you suffered after that. And for what? Only to die.

Derby Day. I let Nadya stay off school, Jill B. came, and we went to the races, Annaliese on my back. If you knew how often your name was on our lips. As usual I had the feeling of going through the motions, of not being "there," while another person registered, even enjoyed, what was going on. I've never seen so many people— so many wealthy, so many dirty people. And the only person who matters was absent. At least I can go to things now. At first I could hardly face the supermarket. I suppose this is what is meant by "getting over it." Not yet, in fact, being better, but learning to present a better face to the world. Literally a better face—the one I see in the mirror has lost some of the haggard look. Funny thing, my face.

The Bible promises the resurrection of the body, doesn't it? I would willingly become a Christian for the sake of your warm body.

Exhausted tonight, but for once not through working myself to a standstill. But I do find it hard to stop. It is as though only by working until I drop can I cope with grief.

I don't include a fraction of what I feel in all these words, words, words. It is a useful safety valve, but I need more than that. I need to stop talking round and round and come up with some conclusions.

Oh, this craving to tell you everything: we won two goldfish at the Derby Fair today; the children all went on the helter-skelter; Annaliese was astonished at all the mangy mongrel dogs; in the morning I did a big shopping and found Spanish orange-blossom honey; and on, and on, and on. Everything, all the insignificant little details which mean nothing to anybody else. The very web and texture of our lives together. I have done almost nothing for years and years that I did not unconsciously relate to you: your approval, disapproval, annoyance, delight. I miss your guidance, your opinions. Even if I could irritate you—never very difficult—it would be something. But no response. Nothing.

What would you think of the way I have carried on since you died? It's a big responsibility. In general, things are still much as when we ran them together. Often, though, I do things I think you might disapprove of. But can I be sure? In life I was often wrong about your reactions. But I have to trust my own judgement, do things my way. No good thinking all the time, "Tony would have done thus and thus."

27

You would have been pleased with today's work, Love. Kind Mr. Germaine's man finished the greenhouse for me. I removed six barrowloads of stale earth and replaced it with about four of fresh. Another two of compost and it will be ready for planting. Tomatoes have been waiting patiently on windowsills and in the cold frame since March. You and I would have finished the greenhouse sooner, but not so well. It's no good without you. No fun. Life is dull. Why did you have to die when we all need you so much? Five of us, all wanting you, and you go and die. Typical of your bloody-mindedness. We have so much before us, such a long road to map out together. I don't want to do it alone, with all these children dependent on me. It's time you did what I want for a change, instead of always going your own wrong-headed way about things. Everything is going to get into the most godawful muddle soon—particularly the money.

I know you were stupid and cruel sometimes, but most of the time it was good. And most of the time is what counts. I notice how ordinary other people's husbands are.

What the hell am I writing all this rubbish for? Where is it supposed to get me? I'm not solving anything by all this writing, and all the day-long brooding. What did I expect? The answer is that nobody knows the answer.

What was it all about then, getting me up at 5:30 in the morning, and out into the garden? It was a very strange compulsion. I knew you were there. What did I expect? Nothing. But you called me and I went. The sun was just a little way above the horizon. It was warm, but fresh. I stood there in my nightie, wondering. I sat down. Nothing happened. Not the first time I have felt strongly compelled to do something I would not normally have done. Something pointless. If you are trying to communicate with me, could you please be a little more clear about it?

I was always right about human relations, but you were right about money. What straits we would be in now if you hadn't "provided for us." And I used to laugh at you. You were right, Love, and thank you.

I'm glad you were cremated. The thought of you disintegrating underground would be horrible. Like Heathcliff, I would have gone to dig you up again, to hold you once more. It was bad enough seeing you dying gradually in the hospital. I wish I had stayed all day and all night with you. I felt I had to make sure the children were all right at night and before school in the mornings.

Lovely flaming June today. I toiled hard in the sunshine, filling the greenhouse with compost and finally planting the tomatoes. I still do these things as if you were coming home soon to admire and criticise. My back is burned red. It's a challenge in a way, making a good life for all of us again.

Just when I think I'm "getting over it," and feel better, even feel a bit guilty that I'm not missing you as much as I did, back it comes. The grief surges through me until I am nothing but a cry for you.

It was a lovely morning. We had breakfast in the garden, at the new table and chairs you bought last year, and at which we sat together perhaps twice last autumn.

In this weather we would be sleeping naked. I

don't miss sex at all—isn't that strange? Never been so long without it since we met, but the thought of it only repels or amuses me. But, oh Love, how I want to lie in your arms!

I'm drinking too much—by my standards, anyway. How dare the sun shine and the flowers bloom and the garden be beautiful when my love is dead! Dead? What does the word mean? He couldn't die without me. We should have died together.

We gave a lot to each other, you and I, looking back over the years. In spite of two black years and one grey one—and even those had their moments—we both did many things that we would never have done alone. Our qualities were complementary. I'm glad it was you I met and married and not someone else, in spite of this tragic end. I resolve that life for the Truman family will not remain dull. For a while, perhaps, until I find my feet. And it can never be so exciting again, but

I'll do my best when I feel sane again. I have to live for two now.

⁓

"An octopus inside me: it squeezed my heart and then crawled to my throat." That's the best description of grief I have read (Anne Phillipe, *No Longer Than a Sigh*). She also says: "Until then I had never been interested in death." Neither had I. I had been sorry often, shed tears sometimes, over the deaths of various people. They had been living and now they were finished. It was often sad, but just as often a release. I never considered the fact of death: What was it about? How do the dead feel? Do they know they are dead? Do they suffer?

Rebecca is sleeping beside me, in your place, as one (or sometimes all) of the children often do. She is a female version of you, quite beautiful. She has caused me problems recently. I realise that she has been trying to compensate herself for losing her daddy, and it does worry me.

I keep going from day to day, sometimes from hour to hour, dealing with things as they arise.

Most people seem to feel that it is the one who continues to live who has the problems, and who is to be pitied. I don't need pity. It's you I'm sorry for. The tragedy is yours, not mine. I have these lovely children, enough money for the time being, the sun shines on me and the nights are warm and clear. One day I hope to break through this barrier of grief and begin to live again. But you don't have another chance. You have lost everything.

And yet there was a moment when I wanted you to die, as I drove the car down Burgh Heath Road and turned into Downs Road that day. It suddenly seemed a simple way out of your struggles, your problems, the dark side of our marriage. Not for long. As the hours, the days and nights dragged by, I longed only for your recovery, in any shape or form. Perhaps for the first time, I really appreciated you. If you had recovered, you old bastard, there's nothing I wouldn't have done for you. There is very little that I wouldn't sacrifice now to have you back for half an hour, for five minutes, to see you smile, talk to you, hear your voice.

Did you want to die? You fought to live, they told me. So many do recover. Why did you have to die, who had so much to live for?

Even now, I don't believe it.

This evening, speeding along the High Street on my bicycle, the cool wind on my skin, I wanted nothing else in the world but to be me. I was—yes—happy. I was free. Since then, I have been suspended, unreal, emotionless. Almost as though I had no more capacity for sorrow or happiness. Something is happening inside me. Sleep. I need sleep.

This evening, sitting and looking out of the window at our now half-wild garden, I thought that it was inconceivable that such a hideous thing had happened to you, and yet there is such a burgeoning of leaves and flowers, such skies and such sun. Because it was horrible, the way you died. It should not have been allowed to happen. I go over and over it in my mind, remembering, remembering.

Annaliese is about as charming as a baby can be. You would adore her. Rebecca said today that you could "look down" and see how sweet she is. I wish I could believe that, my love.

I sprayed the potatoes with Bordeaux mixture, for blight, today. Remember that you did it last year? I had some trouble with the spraying machine.

Have you found out what it all means? If you have, please tell me—if you want to, you will.

Nadya is still in poor health. I got cross with Crispin tonight when he dawdled so long going to bed, and reduced him to tears. I had decided

that things are getting lax without you around.
But I can't really be both of us.

It's terribly late. So tired. Went to a concert.
Missed you to shield me against my ignorance of
music. Went to a party afterwards, but didn't stay
long because of the baby-sitter. I wore a stunning
dress which I have just made and which elicited a
lot of male comment. It's quite pleasant to feel
attractive again. If you were here now we would
be making love, instead of writing this rubbish.

Five months tonight since you died. I have
been writing this for a month and have arrived
nowhere. A few haphazard, egotistical notes.
Oh, my love, I love you. I love you and hate you
and admire you and am irritated by you, just as if
you were still alive.

The kids were lovely today—Sunday, my official birthday. Presents and early morning tea in bed. Then we went (by train, to please Crispin) to Balham to have lunch with Maude. I took a bottle of pseudo-champers I found in the cellar. It transpired that while I was out last night, the kids had got out of bed and iced a cake. When we got home from Maude's, they made me a birthday tea, candles and all. They really do try to make up to me for your absence.

I've drunk everything that was in the cellar and more. That's something else I must stop. From now on I will only drink socially or when absolutely desperate. And I will not write in here again until I have some new ideas.

I've missed writing to you these last few days. It shouldn't have become a habit. You are missing so much and so much, my darling. Annaliese and her little red boots, which she gets out of the boot-box every morning and refuses to be parted from. She stomps around, in this warm weather, often with very little else on, or wearing one boot, or both on the wrong feet.

And what do I say to our little Rebecca when she weeps and weeps and says, "I want my daddy"? I want her daddy, too. You don't stop loving and wanting someone just because they're dead. You can't be dead. There's been some terrible mistake. Tomorrow you will come back and we'll all laugh about it. Am I sorry for myself, for the children, or for you? Tonight I can't tell. The grief is like tummy-ache, you can't analyse it, only put up with it.

You rarely gave me any peace, did you, you old bastard? But a lot of happiness and some suffering and innumerable problems. And you don't give me any peace now. It was beautiful in the garden tonight, almost full moon and the smell of syringa in the warm air. My love, my love, my love, I can't do without you any more.

. . . .

⁓

But the days go by and you don't come. Other people accept it: "Tony Truman's dead. Who's got his job? Who'll chair this meeting, sit on that committee? Poor old Jill, how will she manage with all those children?" Their lives go on and yours doesn't and so they no longer take account of you: you don't exist. But to us your absence is a positive factor; we are affected all the time by the fact that you are not here.

⁓

If I could sleep naked in your arms—any man's arms, perhaps—just sleep, no sex, just feel the comfort of your arms, I could face all the rest on my own. All the problems and tribulations, if I had that nightly peace. The body is so important, the basis of a sound marriage, and what we always came back to, whether things were good or bad between us.

I understand the words "the valley of the shadow of death." It is not one's own death that is to be feared, but the death of one's beloved. I'm sick of being Mother Bloody Courage. I want you.

So I can have all the decisions my way now. Big deal. I'd rather fight you about them every time. I don't like you dead and submissive.

I wish you could have come to Crispin's "open day" at school, or at least been at home when I got back from it. They were all, staff and head, so full of praise for his work and character. We could have glowed together. He is a real support to me in these dark days: so like you—hard and yet soft, aggressive and yet insecure, bossy and organised.

Do you care any more about all these things that I want to discuss with you? Do you know? Are you involved on a new, spiritual plane, where it is unimportant what the children do, or what happens about my car insurance? Or are you wanting to be of help? Are you in fact helping, and does that explain why I'm so "strong" so much of the time?

The trouble with my love for you is that it is so very physical. I endlessly seek comfort in all these books that tell me there is some kind of afterlife. I want so much to believe them. I cannot accept your annihilation. But what I truly want, as I sit alone in the lamplight, reading about spiritualism, Christianity, reincarnation, and all the rest of it, is for you to come behind me and slide your hands under my breasts and kiss me on the lips.

A kind of anesthesia got me through your birthday. And the arrival of Olly: I find that I can't grieve in company. I am getting used to being without you. I don't want to. Come back, my irascible, bloody-minded, much loved love.

I found your scarf behind the washing machine today. The red paisley scarf I gave you, I don't know how many years ago, lying dusty on the floor. So poignant, that scarf in the dust. It's the unexpected I can't cope with. It was much worse than going with the children to put flowers in the churchyard on your birthday. I steeled myself for that.

You are the only real man in my life. The only marvellous proper man. All those others are shadowy projections of you. I wouldn't have had it any other way. Tonight I felt so tired, I felt it would be much easier just to join you, wherever you are or aren't, than to keep slogging on and feeling that I don't do any of it well enough. But other times I want to see it all through. I even

want to have fun again, though I can't see how
that is possible.

I keep promising myself an early night, but
every night I stay up late. And it's not only because there's so much to do. Without you, bed is
just somewhere to sleep. Thank God for sleeping
pills. How would I have survived, with four children to care for, without them? I dread the time
when I shall have to give them up and *really* face
the nights without you. We are off again tomorrow, on another little "holiday." I have to be
alone—the kids don't count—away from all
these people who talk to me.

Since we returned home, I feel quite distant
from you. Contemplated your photograph today
as if it were the face of a stranger. It is half past
midnight and I can't sleep. You don't want to be

forgotten. I don't want to forget you. I'm desperate to remember. I want to hear your voice. I find it hard to recall your voice. I don't want to "get over it." Perversely, I begin to miss my grief. It has been a companion all these months. No substitute for love, but better than nothing.

Certainly, I feel less tense, happier, after so much time alone. I talked to no one but the kids, and they are like extensions of myself. I'm glad that the summer holidays are here and most people will be away most of the time. They are kind, but I don't want companions just now.

Rebecca is sleeping beside me. Her long hair is bleached by the sun. The school holidays are doing her good. She is much better. Crispin too: he sang lustily in the bath tonight, the first time for over six months. Not so Nadya. She is deeply unhappy, but looks in slightly better health. Funny that Rebecca, sleeping there, looks so like you, so very like you, and yet so feminine that the likeness should be impossible.

I don't find any answers to my questions, my longing to know what has happened to you. I can't take the leap into the dark that seems necessary if I am to accept some kind of faith or belief. Anyway, where do I leap to? I wish that you would help me, Love. It was always your way to convert everybody to whatever your latest enthusiasm might be. Such silence makes me think that you must indeed have ceased to exist.

Boiling hot weather. And you have been more than six months dead.

I started writing this because I wanted to tell you about all the things we were doing, about the children's development, the little incidents of family life. But I have devoted very little space to our day-to-day activities, partly because the need to tell you everything has ceased to be so over-powering. Also because it would be quite an impossible task to convey a complete picture of the intricacies of our lives. The daily progress of Annaliese. The exasperation and exhaustion of it all. The unexpected happy moments. If you were absent for a few days, weeks, years even, it would be different. Already we are no longer the family you knew. The trauma of losing you altered us all irrevocably, and we have begun to feel our way toward a new kind of life. I need a new personality to cope with my new situation, and so do they, in other ways. I have to help them. And the baby is a little person now. A tiny human being who does not know what it is to have a father. I hope that somewhere she retains an impression of you, a small memory of some sort to comfort her when she is older.

So I have strayed from my original purpose in writing. What have I written about instead? God knows, but there seems to be a lot of it. Pages and pages of it. Another thing I hoped was that it would enable me to formulate my ideas about life and death. I've failed there, too. I am groping in the dark. Before you died, I was entirely engrossed with the business of day-to-day living, with the exhausting business of sharing a life with you. Now I have to work harder, but I have more time to think. I shall pack in as much living as is possible for someone with all my limitations and responsibilities until the children are launched. Then I would like to join you. I love you, my love. Love and hate you with all the violence I felt when you lived.

Well, I managed the holiday all right, didn't I? Packing and preparing and driving and looking after everything and getting home safely late at night after a hell of a drive. And not despairing, even when Annaliese developed German measles and Nadya's mysterious illness got no better. I admit to a few tears of loneliness and apprehension in the night. And to an ache because you could not see Rebecca looking so happy and tanned and bleached by the sun. . . .

Where do other people get their certainties, and why don't I feel any?

I can see that if we hadn't had hard times in the past, I would not be able to cope so well now. I owe so much to you—the good and the bad. And our love which withstood everything and never quite gave way. I could never give or receive love like that again. Lucky to have it once in a lifetime. Bully for me, then; I'll manage. But what about you? I can't let that question go. You may be suffering torments much worse than mine. I don't want to make demands on you, I want you to be at peace. You were never at peace in life, were you?

Those hours and hours and days and years we wasted together, and never discussed those things I long to ask you now. But how could we? The questions that haunt me now presuppose your illness and death. If I could have just one of those hours back. Five minutes, even. Two minutes, just to hold your hand.

I have now, after that incredibly hot week in Cromer, acquired the best suntan of my life. Would you be glad to see me looking well, or does it gratify the dead to see their beloved as walking embodiments of grief? Or don't you give a damn? Nadya is better since we got home. I think that she is desperately insecure. Another good reason for not moving house too soon.

I am suspended between past and future. The present is a void.

I wonder how all this will read in, say, ten years? As meaningless, superficial and self-indulgent, I expect. But it is a compulsion as necessary as alcohol to the alcoholic: just now I grabbed this notebook as though it were a bottle for which I thirsted, fought back the tears because the pen was missing and I needed to write. Found it under the bed—Annaliese's work, no doubt. Already I feel calmer, after this thirst-quenching paragraph.

I think I would weep more about your death if only it were not for this constant feeling that it hasn't happened. Tomorrow I will wake up from the nightmare. That is what keeps the pain at a distance so much of the time. And yet, at other levels I do accept it and make the many adjustments that are necessary in our lives. I hate being five in the family. It's such an ugly number.

Sometimes I feel guilty that I am not grieving

enough, the burden is temporarily lifted and I feel quite cheerful. Then, unpredictably, something happens to remind me, and the heartache returns. But it is no longer a constant obsession. I no longer wait impatiently for visitors to go so that I can be alone to grieve. I can even contemplate the possibility of evening classes or theatre visits in the autumn.

Why feel guilty? I'm glad that I don't feel the need to wallow in self-pity. I am not to be pitied. Though it isn't going to be easy bringing up the four children alone. It is probably just as well that I can't foresee the difficulties that lie ahead. Then there is the problem of what to do with my own life, since I have to go on living. I musn't waste it, but there is no cause to which I feel I must dedicate myself, I have no talent which I should exploit. I am so ordinary and so bogged down with responsibilities that time will probably just pass and I'll achieve nothing.

I don't fear death itself, but I fear a violent or painful death. Coward. You went through it, so I can. How much did you suffer, my love? The worst of the pain seemed to be over by the last Tuesday. You were so drugged by then, I hope that you couldn't feel anything more. But you hated the ignominy of sickness. You idiot! As though it mattered—you made it so much harder for yourself. I hope the pain wasn't too bad.

You shouldn't have died with so much undecided, unfinished, unreconciled. If only for that, I hope that there is some afterlife, so that you can finish sorting yourself out. But how will you do it without me to help you? I provided the continuity and tenacity, you provided the excitement.

I feel so close to you, so near to an understanding, as if only the dimness of the moonlight prevented me from seeing the truth with absolute clarity. What should I do to understand?

Immortality is wishful thinking. I don't want to lose you.

How dismal living is, and how difficult to know what to do for the best, what to think and believe. It can't have all been for nothing. If it were, you were cheated.

The house-martins are beginning to line up ready to fly away. And you weren't here when they arrived. You missed the end of winter and hopeful spring and one of the longest, hottest summers ever. All you saw was the first few early snowdrops. I'll never be able to see snowdrops with dry eyes again. And springs and summers will come and go, and you will be forgotten, and it is not to be borne.

Most of the time I do bear it, though. How? Occupational therapy—not difficult in my circumstances. By anesthetising myself, and leaving the puppet to perform for me.

If only I could do something for you. It was so easy when you were alive: meals when you were hungry, sex when you lusted, succor when you were ill. All I can do now is weep inwardly and wonder what has become of you. I can bring up your children, your lovely, exasperating children, but only to the best of my very limited ability. I can ensure that they treasure what memories they have of you. But that's so little.

This projected move to Bristol: How can I cope?

⁂

I want to sleep in your arms.

⁂

Now I am trying to plan a future for us all, without you. Have I stopped being so obsessional about the past, having to go over and over every detail of our relationship? I think so. In spite of (because of?) the struggles and imperfections, meeting and loving you was the best thing that ever happened to me. I have nothing to complain about: it was you, my unquiet love, my restless and dissatisfied lover, who suffered and suffered so, and in the end lost everything.

I fear the prospect of moving home and family alone. If I make a wrong decision, I bear all the responsibility alone. I'm a coward and brave at the same time. What would you think about my plan? I ask myself over and over. "I have no compass now" (Kathleen Raine). No compass.

How long and soundly I used to sleep in your arms, and with what difficulty did I rouse myself in the mornings. Now the nights are long and wakeful. If you have something to say, it is up to me to do all I can to try to understand, because there is no one else to listen to you. Keep it up, my darling. I am tuned in to frequencies I didn't know existed, a world I don't know how to reach.

I'll reject nothing, but explore every which way and keep my sensibilities alert always.

About time I really got to grips with my financial situation. I'll manage. If I don't do anything stupid, I'll manage.

Did my desire for revenge kill you? Was I the cause of that horrible suffering in the hospital? If there were a God, and he were any use, he would give us another chance.

It suddenly seems so long ago, our life together, our love. It is receding and I desperately try to grab it back, to hang on to the memories, but the immediacy is gone. How can I accept that you belong to the past, you who were always so positively, so vitally THERE?

It's been so long. A lot of the time, I seem to be waiting—for some revelation, some understanding. What the hell do I expect—you to appear in a flash of blue light and explain to me the mysteries of eternity? At other times I just get on with life, quite cheerfully now, dealing with all the problems as they occur. Then, suddenly, I'm gripped by terror. All the responsibility is mine. How the hell do I keep going? No wonder I'm exhausted most of the time. But the strength to go on seems to come from somewhere. I'm paying for taking you for granted all these years, not appreciating you enough.

Tomorrow you will have been dead for eight months. It is inconceivable that I have managed without you for so long. And yet not without you. I live with the results of your actions, your personality. I myself am partly the result of what you were. And the children. Although it is only a few months since I last spoke to you, I seem to have been writing these ridiculous notes for years. It's a compulsion and a drug.

Sometimes I feel as though I have become as hard as nails: nothing will move me again. I have been through the worst and I don't care and I'm not weeping.

I no longer think that *everything* people say is uninteresting. But I do get tired of the monstrous importance that they attach to little things, those who have not known grief. I mustn't think of myself as one of an elite, but it certainly sets one apart in many ways, perhaps in every way. I will never be the same again.

If I don't accept the fact of your death, deep inside me, I won't be able to carry on. It comes and goes, this "hardness." Sometimes the smallest things touch me.

The children mention you often, but it is

weeks since even Rebecca wept for you. They have accepted their situation as a fatherless family. I am pleased (and take some of the credit?) for the fact that the transition has been made; yet, at the same time, hurt that they can do without you.

I show the world a confidence that I don't feel. If the move to Bristol happens, it will certainly be a branching off into a life of my own, and it could be an absolute disaster.

Planning to leave this house—it's like deserting you.

Stormy in the garden tonight. Trees tossing, wind and rain, shreds of torn cloud across the black sky. It made me think of you in your difficult moods. No more hope of changing you than of changing the weather.

Do you approve of the move to Bristol? I feel enthusiastic, light in spirit, normal in a way that I have not been for God knows how long. How I miss you, long for your warmth in the night.

I've done the one unforgivable thing for the English—showed emotion in public. First visit to the theatre since you died. Real emotion in that temple of synthetic emotion. In the foyer, after the play was over. Everybody pretended not to notice, but how embarrassed they were. But how could it all happen without you there? I knew all over again that you were dead.

Exactly nine months since I last kissed your warm lips, already lifeless. Where were you then? Where are you now? Why did you leave me to suffer like this?

I am less obsessed by you. Misery comes in huge splashing waves, and ebbs, and life goes forward. I have even had a lover, and enjoyed it, although I wept for you in his arms, poor man.

I should stop writing this, unless it helps me reach some clearer understanding. What is the position now: the children accept the situation—not gladly, but they accept it—and life goes on. In some ways family life is easier and in others much, much harder. I grieve less, am less lost, eat more, plan more, and even "live" a little. When I look at your life, which I knew so well, if not entirely, I can discern no pattern, no purpose; neither is there any in your death. I accept the possibility of some form of afterlife or continued existence—of what kind I don't know, but assume it to be beyond my imagination to comprehend. In some ways it would be easier to accept your complete annihilation, because it is the touch of your warm, firm, beautiful hands that I want, not some spiritual presence.

~~~

What a frightful day! Tense and irritable, with that awful ringing in my ears that I've had for months, louder than ever. I shrieked at the kids and felt no pleasure in our little one.

~~~

The children were so kind tonight. Bonfire night. When I failed so miserably at the bonfire (it wouldn't light), Nadya said that she wished Daddy were here, and the other two shushed her and assured me that I was doing very well, several times. Rebecca even said at bedtime, rather hollowly, that I was "much better at it."

~~~

The Baby says "Da-dee" when she sees your photograph. Bless her. It's too cruel.

I slept soundly last night, and with very little drug. First time. I'll be able to give up the pills completely soon.

What a happy baby Annaliese is. She has been our saving joy.

Pure sensuous passion with my lover in the firelight. Not a scrap of love in it. And I slept without drugs.

What a terrible thought, just now, by the dying embers of the fire: I began wondering what you and I had been doing exactly a year ago. Then the thought struck me that I *would not go back*. Forgive me.

And there was also a small spark of pride in my

new independence and the tiny movement towards a new life which I have recently made. You liked me strong and independent, or so you said.

I have been wondering, too, what you would have wanted for me if you could have foreseen your death. First and obviously you wanted me not to have financial worries while the children were small. I think we shall be okay if I am sensible, though inflation is undermining your plans. Secondly, you would want me to provide a happy home for the children and help them to exploit their talents to the full. I'll have to follow my instinct and trust my judgement in that. It puts considerable limitations on what I might choose to do with my life, limitations which I gladly accept. Of course, you would want to be remembered by us all, loved, longed for, but would you want us to continue with the agonies of grief? Or would you want me to find happiness and your so-vivid personality to become just a memory? If grieving is the only way that you can remain part of my life, I would rather grieve than be happy. Yet I often want to feel carefree again, light of heart and of foot. Is it possible to reconcile these two conflicting desires?

This has got me nowhere. I wish, wish, WISH that there was something I could do for *you*.

Resentfully, today, I thought: "I shall never feel happy again." Never feel love either. Or if I do feel these things, it will be because I have forgotten you.

Why this feeling of suspense that I have felt ever since you died? Waiting for you to come back, perhaps? For me to join you? For my new life to begin? All three, perhaps. Or waiting to awaken from the nightmare?

I haven't written anything for days, or is it weeks? The passage of time has become meaningless. The last eleven months have vanished like a sigh. I manage to keep sufficient grasp on time to remember to keep most appointments, to get the children to school, but, for the rest, I am groping about in a time-fog.

The reason for not writing is that, not for the first time, but more devastatingly and totally and for longer, I have stopped feeling anything. Nothing can touch me again, neither happiness nor sorrow. In a way it is worse than the agonies of grief. What have I become?

＊＊＊

How poignantly you were with us, this evening when we decorated the Christmas tree. Almost a year. I wept again, so I am not completely stone. Oh my love, all the living people in the world are less alive than you are.

1986

The $letter$ was my lifeline, my regular communication with a man whom the rest of the world considered to be dead. Then one night I put it in the cupboard at my bedside as usual when I had finished writing, and it stayed there for seven years. By chance, I never threw it away. We moved house, the children grew, the world changed and so did I. It was only when my good friend Lionel was suffering because of the death of his best friend that I recalled my own desperate need to relate to other people who had experienced something similar, as well as the total lack of satisfactory reading material on the subject. I looked to see if the letter was still there. It was. The old exercise book filled with familiar handwriting—but where was the stranger who had written it?

I did not at all want to be reacquainted with my past self, and it was weeks before I could immunise myself sufficiently to type out a copy and give it to my friend. Although subsequent events have convinced me that people in that solitary limbo called bereavement find the letter a help and comfort, I still feel uneasy about it. Now that it is to be published, I would like to say to any woman who finds herself suddenly, unbelievably, in the position I was in all those years ago: It will be okay. Just keep putting one foot in front of the other, day after day, and you can survive. You can be happy again. But it may be more different than you could possibly imagine.

What kept me going? The children, of course. Friends. A kind doctor and solicitor at a crucial time. Tony's practical foresight, and the welfare state. Another bedrock support has been the growth of the women's movement, and especially the peace camp at Greenham Common. People often ask me if I am a feminist: a widow with four children either adopts a feminist approach or accepts the second-class status offered by society. The only other option would be to rejoin the patriarchy by marrying again. But I have developed a taste for freedom during my years alone. I like men as friends, colleagues, lovers—but not as husbands. Perhaps we outgrow marriage, or perhaps our society has outgrown it. Or maybe I personally have made a virtue of necessity.

How have we all fared? The children are wonderful. I admire their attitudes, their courage in this corrupt and cruel world which we have forced them to inhabit. Three of them are now embarking on adult life, the fourth still has several more years of secondary school to complete before my responsibilities begin to diminish. They all cope as well as, if not better than, their contemporaries from two-parent families. As for me, I commenced irregular, ill-paid, part-time work when Annaliese was three. When she was four, I did a post-graduate year in drama at Bristol University. But I was not exactly an employer's dream: I lacked confidence, credibility, experience, youth, someone to care for the children while I was at work. A full-time job has continued to elude me. However, a combination of lodgers, part-time teaching, part-time arts administration, and now part-time writing has helped to keep us afloat. I may again be making a virtue of necessity, but I enjoy the combination that has evolved: it is flexible, rarely boring, and a challenge, if hardly lucrative.

I have learnt the danger of expecting security, or desiring it too much. Or, having achieved it, trying to hang on to it. And once I had discounted the probability of a secure future, whole new vistas opened up. There are times when I envy the apparently stable relationships, high salaries, safe jobs, and comfortable pensions which some people I know take for granted. What have I got instead? Loneliness, erratic income, unpredictable future? Maybe a little more understanding than I had in "safer" days? Is independence worth the price? I think so. But maybe I have just been lucky so far.

Our marriage was so intense. We never reached a level, easygoing plateau of affection. It was all heights and depths, extremes of love and hate, desire, happiness, suffering—leaving, for me at least, energy for little else, or so it seems now. This closeness, obsession almost, left a huge void when he died. For about three years, though coping on the surface, I ached for him. Then there was a reversion. I began to have nightmares. I dreamed that he returned in various ways, and that I did not want him back. I would wake in the morning feeling as though I had been killing him over and over again. I felt guilt, bitterness, resentment. All the negative parts of our relationship surfaced. Our life together seemed to have been a lie. During the days, I was occupied with struggling with my new life, new problems, new relationships, new happiness even, but at night the old problems returned, unresolved. Perhaps I never will get it all straight. I have come to no conclusions about our relationship, about marriage as an institution, about the significance, if any, of living and dying. I distrust people who are certain about these things. I think I have lost my fear of death: if he could go through with it, so can I.

Strangely, it is as though I have inherited his restlessness, his intolerance, his divine discontent, all of which have been of real assistance during the darker times. Similarly, I feel often that I "live for two." Anything beautiful or harmonious—a cool bright night or a sparkling morning, a building, a view—has twice its previous poignancy. I offer no explanations, simply accept such things and get on with a life which continues to be filled with hard work, interesting and rewarding.

Yet his absence will always overshadow our lives. His untimely and unnecessary death remains a tragedy for his parents, for us, and above all for him. Even after all these years, from time to time something will remind me, and I want to double up with the physical pain of it. An effort of will, and seconds later the spasm has passed. Nobody noticed. Life goes on. The impossible fact of his death remains.

Jill Truman
September 1986